# EXTREME!

# Gravity-Defying Stunt Spectaculars

## Paul Harrison

Capstone
press

Mankato, Minnesota

**Safety advice**
The stunts described in this book are
dangerous and should only be carried
out by trained professionals. Do not
attempt any of them yourself.

Fact Finders is published by Capstone Press,
a Capstone Publishers company.
151 Good Counsel Drive, P.O. Box 669,
Mankato, Minnesota 56002.
www.capstonepress.com

Library of Congress Cataloging-in-Publication Data

Harrison, Paul, 1969-
  Gravity-defying stunt spectaculars / by Paul Harrison,
Amanda Robbins.
  p. cm. -- (Fact finders. extreme adventures!)
  Includes bibliographical references and index.
  Summary: "Describes various life-threatening stunts,
including tight-rope walking, BASE jumping, and human
cannonballs"--Provided by publisher.
  ISBN 978-1-4296-4555-3 (library binding)
  ISBN 978-1-4296-4617-8 (pbk.)
1. Tricks--Juvenile literature. 2. Daredevils--Juvenile
literature. 3. Stunt performers--Juvenile literature.  I.
Robbins, Amanda. II. Title.

GV1548.H37 2010
796.04'6--dc22

2009027857

Produced for A & C Black by
MONKEY PUZZLE MEDIA LTD
Monkey Puzzle Media Ltd
48 York Avenue
Hove BN3 1PJ, UK

Editor: Susie Brooks
Design: Mayer Media Ltd
Picture research: Lynda Lines
Series consultants: Jane Turner and James de Winter

This book is produced using paper that is made from
wood grown in managed, sustainable forests. It is natural,
renewable, and recyclable. The logging and manufacturing
processes conform to the environmental regulations of the
country of origin.

Printed in Malaysia by Tien Wah Press (Pte.) Ltd

102009
005558

Picture acknowledgements
Alamy p. 26–27 (Jacob Ammentorp Lund); Bigfoot 4X4 Inc
p. 9 top; Corbis pp. 1 (CSPA/NewSport), 4–5 (Jason Lee/
Reuters), 12 top (CSPA/NewSport), 21 (Hulton-Deutsch
Collection), 24 left (Hulton-Deutsch Collection); Discovery
Films/BBC p. 15; Getty Images pp. 6, 14, 17 (Colin
Meagher), 18–19 (AFP), 22–23, 28 left (AFP); MPM
Images pp. 5 top, 10; PAPhotos p. 23 (François Mori/AP);
Photolibrary.com pp. 20 (Sundell Joakim), 28–29 (Max
Dereta); Reuters p. 11 (Brendan McDermid); Rex Features
pp. 7 bottom (ITV), 8–9 (Kip Rano), 12–13 (Everett
Collection), 24–25 (EDPICS/Bill Smith); Ronald Grant
Archive p. 7 top; Sony Pics/Everett p. 26 left; Topfoto.co.uk
pp. 16 (ImageWorks), 18 (UPP).

The front cover shows a stuntman performing at the
World Stunt Awards in Los Angeles, California (Corbis/
Mario Anzuoni/Reuters).

Every effort has been made to contact copyright holders
of material reproduced in this book. Any omissions will
be rectified in subsequent printings if notice is given to the
publishers.

# CONTENTS

All aboard 4

Silent stars 6

Leaping loonies 8

Water torture 10

Crazy cars 12

High jinks 14

Over the edge 16

Free fall 18

The wall of death 20

Get a grip 22

The human cannonball 24

Cheap thrills 26

Free as a bird 28

Glossary 30

Further information 31

Index 32

**Abbreviations** **km** stands for kilometers • **m** stands for meters • **ft** stands for feet • **km/h** stands for kilometers per hour • **mph** stands for miles per hour

# All aboard

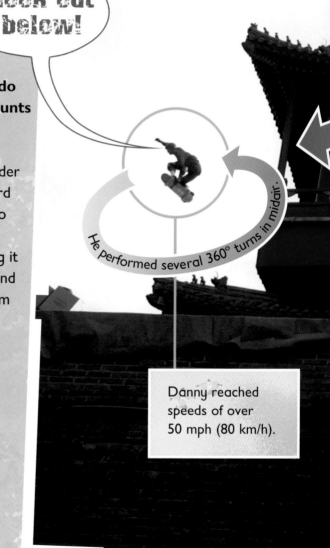

*Danny Way clears the Great Wall of China on a skateboard in 2005.*

**Look out below!**

**Any half-decent skateboarder can show off with a few tricks—but what do the top riders do? They make their stunts bigger and better than anyone else's!**

Skateboard stunts are a battle between rider and science. As soon as a skater and board get off the ground, **gravity** does its best to pull them back down again. Gravity will always win—but there are ways of making it wait. Big ramps help riders travel higher and faster, so gravity takes longer to drag them back to earth with a crunch.

*He performed several 360° turns in midair.*

Danny reached speeds of over 50 mph (80 km/h).

## Clear air

**The Big Air skateboard competition features riders using a 62-foot (19-meter) tall ramp called the Mega Ramp.**

**gravity** a force that attracts objects to each other, especially toward Earth

1,600 ft (500 m) down!

Danny flew 79 ft (24 m) high over the wall.

▲ Bob Burnquist **grinds** along a rail into the Grand Canyon in 2006. He is wearing a parachute for a safe landing.

Even the cops were fascinated!

Danny used a huge ramp to give him enough energy to get over the wall.

**grind** to ride a skateboard down a rail

# Silent stars

**Modern movie stunts look really extreme thanks to computer trickery. But in the early days of film there were no computers to help out. All the stunts were done for real!**

*It looks as if Harold Lloyd is hanging high over the street, but the camera angle hides a ledge just below him.*

An old-fashioned stunt was a bit like a magic trick. The idea was not to let the audience see how it was done. Silent movie stars such as Buster Keaton and Harold Lloyd knew how to make stunts work. Clever planning and **camera angles** were the keys to making a stunt look much more dangerous than it really was.

Gulp!

## Thrillers!

Harold Lloyd's films became known as "thrill comedies" thanks to his extreme stunts.

**camera angle** the position of a camera in relation to the subject

Buster Keaton seems sure to be flattened, but he's done his math.

Keaton has measured the height of the window.

This tells him exactly how far away to stand.

Keaton stands exactly where the open window lands.

Phew!

# Leaping loonies

Motorcycles and monster trucks aren't meant to fly, but that doesn't stop people from trying to get them **airborne**!

*Stunt rider Evel Knievel jumps a row of London buses in 1975.*

The angle of the takeoff ramp and the power of the engine give the bike speed.

Gravity pulls the bike downward.

**airborne** carried through the air

*With enough speed and a ramp, even monster trucks can fly.*

If it goes wrong, the bike lands here.

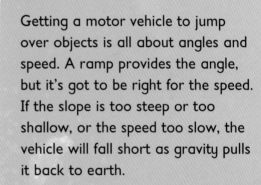

Getting a motor vehicle to jump over objects is all about angles and speed. A ramp provides the angle, but it's got to be right for the speed. If the slope is too steep or too shallow, or the speed too slow, the vehicle will fall short as gravity pulls it back to earth.

# Long jumper!

In March 2008, Robbie Maddison jumped a whopping 346 feet (105 meters) on a motorcycle—a new world record.

# Water torture

*Harry Houdini amazed audiences with his scary underwater escape tricks.*

**Holding your breath for a long time underwater feels like torture. Your lungs fill with carbon dioxide, and it's only a matter of time before you become unconscious. How long do you think you could last?**

Most people can hold their breath for no more than a minute. But some performers and **free divers** can last much longer than this. They train themselves in special techniques, such as drawing **oxygen** from other parts of the body toward the lungs. Staying calm also helps people to use less oxygen, but that's difficult when you know you could possibly drown.

## Staying underwater

If divers gulp pure oxygen—a technique known as oxygen loading—before they dive, they can stay underwater for longer.

**carbon dioxide** waste gas we breathe out    **free divers** people who dive without air tanks

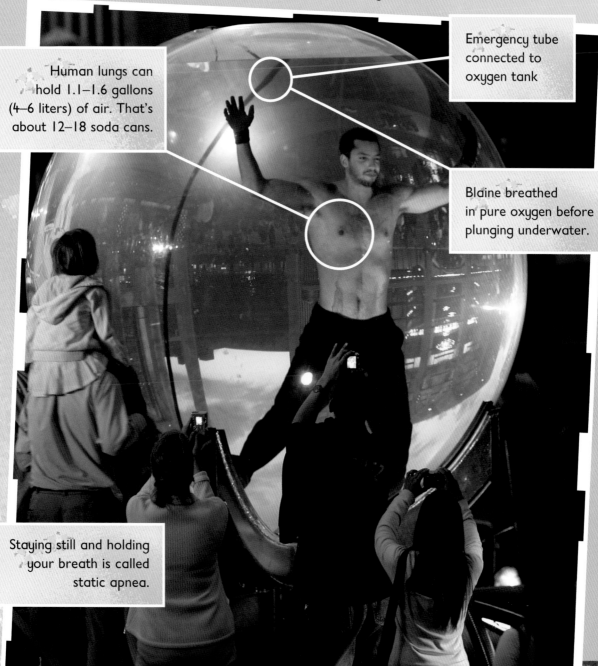

David Blaine sets a new world breath-holding record of 17 minutes 4.4 seconds.

Human lungs can hold 1.1–1.6 gallons (4–6 liters) of air. That's about 12–18 soda cans.

Emergency tube connected to oxygen tank

Blaine breathed in pure oxygen before plunging underwater.

Staying still and holding your breath is called static apnea.

**oxygen** gas that humans need for survival

# Crazy cars

If your car skidded, spun or rolled over onto its roof, you'd fail your driving test. But this is everyday work for a stunt driver.

"Spiderman" jumps from one car to the other.

Balancing on two wheels is difficult because you are driving on such a thin strip of tire.

## Don't brake!

A lot of stunt driving is about keeping going. If you don't, gravity gets the better of you and pulls you down to the ground.

The average family car weighs around 3,300 pounds (1,500 kilograms) and is designed to drive on four wheels—but that doesn't mean it has to. Cars can jump 200 feet (61 meters) over obstacles, do **barrel rolls** in midair and even go skiing—that's whizzing along on two wheels, not the winter sport!

*Superspy James Bond performs his famous barrel roll stunt in* The Man with the Golden Gun.

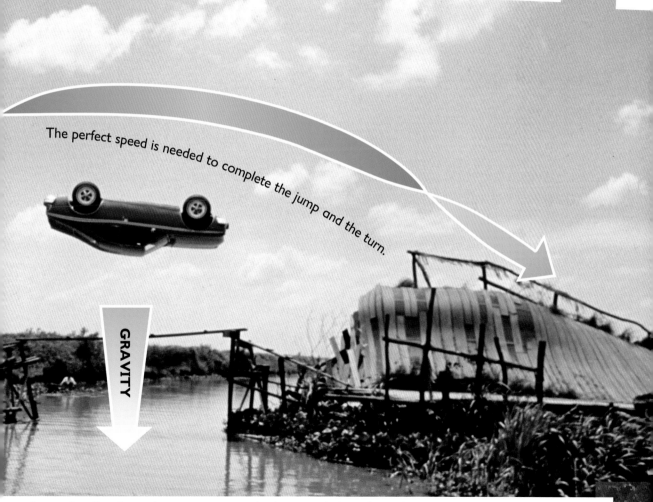

The perfect speed is needed to complete the jump and the turn.

GRAVITY

**barrel roll**  where the car spins upside down and then the right way up in midair

# High jinks

Imagine tiptoeing across a wire that's narrower than your foot—with nothing on either side and a knee-knocking drop below. Welcome to the world of tightrope walking!

People have walked tightropes in the most extreme locations—across **ravines**, between skyscrapers and even over Niagara Falls. At King's Island, Ohio, a record-breaking walker managed 2,000 feet (609 meters) across a high wire. Long tightropes like this wobble and sag, making it much harder to keep your balance. Stumble, and there's only one way to go—down.

*Tightrope-walking legend Charles Blondin crosses Niagara Falls carrying his manager, Harry Colcord, on his back.*

## Fun times

The correct name for tightrope walking is funambulism.

**ravine** a deep, narrow valley between two cliffs

*In 1974, Philippe Petit walked between two skyscrapers in New York wearing the world's widest flared pants!*

Crosswinds make balancing more difficult.

Petit's stunt lasted for 45 minutes.

A pole helps Petit balance.

GRAVITY

**crosswinds** winds that blow from the side

# Over the edge

*Annie Edson Taylor was the first person to go over Niagara Falls in a barrel—at age 63!*

**Big waterfalls look spectacular and are supremely dangerous. So why would anyone want to float over the edge of one?**

Going over the edge of a waterfall isn't difficult. The hard part is surviving. Large waterfalls can drop over 100 feet (30 meters) into churning waters and dangerous **currents** below. But whooshing over falls in a barrel or **kayak** isn't as crazy as it seems. Both are **buoyant**, meaning they will quickly float back up to the surface—and you have more chance of living if you don't sink too far.

## Whoosh!

More than 6 million cubic feet (170,000 cubic meters) of water rush over the crest of Niagara Falls every minute.

**current** the flow of water **kayak** a canoe with a covered top

Water shoots off top of cliff

Kayaker shoots off waterfall into the air

The kayaker's paddling speed has taken him farther out than the water. But he cannot resist gravity for long!

Helmet protects the kayaker in case of a rocky landing.

GRAVITY

Kayak is sealed to lock in air. This makes it lighter than water, so it will bob afloat when it lands.

*An extreme sports fan gets his thrills in a waterfall.*

**buoyant** able to float

# Free fall

You pay a lot of money to jump out of an airplane with a parachute. But BASE jumpers don't bother with a plane—they just throw themselves from a high object instead.

There are two more big differences between normal parachuting and BASE jumping. First, surprise crosswinds and **updrafts** can whistle around objects such as cliffs and buildings, and these affect the parachute. Second, BASE jumpers usually have less time to open their chute. If they get it wrong, they won't live to regret it.

*BASE jumpers celebrate the opening of the world's tallest building in Taiwan.*

## All in the name

The letters in BASE stand for:

B—Buildings

A—Aerials

S—Spans (e.g. bridges)

E—Earth (e.g. mountains)

**updraft** wind blowing upward

At this moment, a BASE jumper hopes he's packed his parachute properly!

UPDRAFT

**Air resistance** stops jumpers from falling any faster than 120 mph (193 km/h).

AIR RESISTANCE

Gravity is stronger than updraft and air resistance put together.

GRAVITY

**air resistance** the way air slows objects down as they move

# The wall of death

**Riding a motorcycle upside down or sideways around the walls of a huge barrel seems impossible. So how do riders defy nature and live to tell the tale?**

Wall-of-death rides became popular fairground attractions in the 1930s. Sometimes the riders took passengers with them. Imagine being picked out of the crowd for that!

The trick to cheating gravity in the wall of death is simple—sheer speed. As long as the bike is moving fast enough, the rider will not end up in a heap on the floor.

*Though it looks dangerous, the hardest thing about riding a globe of death like this is not hitting other people.*

## Roaring on

Lions, monkeys, and bears have all ridden the wall of death as passengers in cars. So who's driving...?

**force** a push or a pull on an object, making it move or change shape

A daring spectator becomes part of the show in this wall-of-death stunt.

The bike's speed produces **force** that pushes the tires against the wall.

Here we go!

SPEED

GRAVITY

# Get a grip

When we want to get to the top of a building, we use the stairs or an elevator. Extreme stunt lovers prefer to climb up the outside—without using ropes!

*Alain Robert is the world's most famous free climber.*

Chalk bag for drying hands

**Hurry up and take the photo!**

It's a long, long way to fall.

Alain pushes his feet and knees against the wall for grip.

**vertigo** a feeling of dizziness    **urban** describes a built-up area, such as a town or city

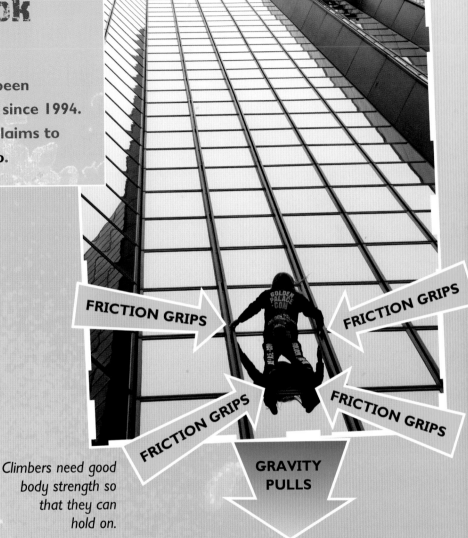

# Don't look down!

Alain Robert has been climbing buildings since 1994. Unbelievably, he claims to suffer from **vertigo**.

FRICTION GRIPS

FRICTION GRIPS

FRICTION GRIPS

FRICTION GRIPS

GRAVITY PULLS

*Climbers need good body strength so that they can hold on.*

Scrambling up buildings without using ropes is called **urban** free climbing. Getting a good grip is really important, so sweaty hands are very bad news. Climbers use chalk powder to keep their hands as dry as possible. This gives them some **friction** to prevent a slippery fall.

**friction** the force that slows movement between two objects rubbing together

# The human cannonball

Cannons are for wars. Aren't they? Yes—but some people are so desperate to fly that they are willing to be fired like a cannonball!

BANG! A human cannonball takes to the air.

A spring inside the cannon fires out the cannonball.

Energy carries the cannonball upward.

Smoke makes the cannon look real.

The human cannonball act is a combination of stunt work and science. Before being blasted through the air, the cannonballs need to know both the angle of their flight and their speed. This tells them how far away to put the catching net. If they mess up the math, they're in for a painful landing.

# Spring loaded

The cannon isn't a real cannon. Rather than using gunpowder to propel the cannonball, a big spring is used.

*The human cannonball somersaults in the air to land on his back in the net.*

Gravity pulls downward on the cannonball— and wins in the end!

# Cheap thrills

Runner judges the gap.

**Running around town is one thing— but some people take it to a whole new level! Free running, or *parkour*, is a sport that doesn't let walls or buildings get in its way.**

Free running is all about getting from one place to another—fast. Instead of going around things, the runner jumps, swings, or climbs over obstacles. A good sense of balance is essential as many of the moves are acrobatic. **Spatial awareness** is also handy, so runners don't misjudge a gap and fall.

*Free running was featured in the James Bond film* Casino Royale.

**spatial awareness** knowing where you are in relation to objects around you

Leaping over gaps takes fitness, balance, and a good sense of distance and height.

Defeats gravity to head for a perfect landing on the wall.

ENERGY

Runner's arms and legs help him balance in the air.

GRAVITY

# Buzz on balance

A person's balance is controlled by **sensors** inside the ear. That's why ear infections can make people feel dizzy.

**sensors** things that pick up information such as movement, light, or heat

# Free as a bird

**People have often dreamed of soaring through the skies like birds. But we've always needed bulky equipment or aircraft to do it. Until now . . .**

Our arms aren't strong enough to flap wings successfully, but a wing suit can make it feel as if we're flying. A wing suit has cloth panels between the legs and arms, which make the wearer's **surface area** bigger. This increases air resistance, slowing the fall and allowing the person to **glide** like a bird.

*Swiss inventor Yves Rossy has developed a jet-powered personal wing, capable of traveling at over 180 mph (290 km/h).*

**surface area** the size of something on the outside

# Natural solution

Some animals, such as flying squirrels, have flaps of skin, like a wing suit. This helps them soar from tree to tree.

Wing suits increase air resistance.

Air resistance slows the fallers...

... but gravity still pulls harder.

**glide** to fly smoothly through the air without a source of power

# Glossary

**airborne** carried through the air

**air resistance** the way air slows objects down as they move

**barrel roll** where the car spins upside down and then the right way up in midair

**buoyant** able to float

**camera angle** the position of a camera in relation to the subject

**carbon dioxide** the waste gas that we breathe out

**crosswinds** winds that blow from the side

**current** the flow of water

**force** a push or a pull on an object, making it move or change shape

**free divers** people who dive without air tanks

**friction** the force that slows movement between two objects rubbing together

**glide** to fly smoothly through the air without a source of power

**gravity** a force that attracts objects to each other, especially toward Earth

**grind** to ride a skateboard down a rail

**kayak** a canoe with a covered top, paddled with a double-headed oar

**oxygen** gas that humans need for survival

**ravine** a deep, narrow valley between two cliffs

**sensors** things that pick up information such as movement, light, or heat

**spatial awareness** knowing where you are in relation to objects around you

**surface area** the size of something on the outside

**updraft** wind blowing upward

**urban** describes a built-up area, such as a town or city

**vertigo** a feeling of dizziness

# Further information

## Books

Deciding which are the best stunts ever attempted could be argued about until the end of time. One author puts down his top ten in *The World's Most Dangerous Stunts* by Tim O'Shei (Edge Books, 2006)

Another book featuring spectacular stunts along with interviews and statistics and facts is *Yikes! Scariest Stunts Ever!* by Jesse Leon McCann (Scholastic, 2006)

## Web sites

FactHound offers a safe, fun way to find Internet sites related to this book. All of the sites on FactHound have been researched by our staff. Visit *www.facthound.com* for age-appropriate sites. You may browse subjects by clicking on letters, or by clicking on pictures and words.
**FactHound will fetch the best sites for you!**

## Films

*Ben-Hur* directed by William Wyler (MGM, 1959)
A story of revenge set in Roman times. The most famous scene is a thrilling chariot race. There is a rumor that a stuntman actually died filming this scene, but it's not true.

*Raiders of the Lost Ark* directed by Stephen Spielberg (Paramount Pictures, 1981)
All-action archaeologist Indiana Jones battles the Nazis to get the Ark of the Covenant. There's a famous fight scene on a moving truck.

*The World Is Not Enough* directed by Michael Apted (MGM, 1999)
Superspy James Bond foils terrorist plots and manages to make a motorboat do a barrel roll in this action-packed thriller.

# Index

air resistance 19, 28, 29
angles 6, 8, 9, 25

balance 14, 15, 26, 27
barrel rolls 13
BASE jumping 18–19
Big Air competition 4
breath-holding 10, 11

camera tricks 6
carbon dioxide 10
car stunts 12–13
climbing 22–23
computers 6

divers 10

energy 5, 24, 27

film 6
flight 25
floating 16, 17
force 20, 21

free climbing 22, 23
free divers 10
free running 26–27
friction 23
funambulism 14

gliding 28
gravity 4, 8, 9, 12, 13, 17,
    19, 20, 21, 25, 27, 29

human cannonball 24–25

kayak 16, 17

lungs 10, 11

Mega Ramp 4
monster trucks 8, 9
motorbikes 8, 9, 20
motor vehicles 9
movie stunts 6–7

oxygen 10, 11

parachute 5, 18, 19
parkour 26

ramps 4, 5, 8, 9

skateboarding 4–5
spatial awareness 26
speed 4, 8, 9, 13, 17, 20,
    21, 25
stunt drivers 12
surface area 28

tightrope walking 14–15
trucks 8, 9

underwater stunts 10–11
updraft 18, 19

vertigo 22, 23

wall of death 20–21
waterfalls 16–17
wing suit 28–29